THE
LAUREL & HARDY
POSTER BOOK

**THE
LAUREL & HARDY
POSTER BOOK**

A ZACHARY KWINTNER BOOK

Text and design copyright © 1991 Zachary Kwintner Books Ltd.

ISBN 1 872532 34 9

The publishers would like to thank BFI Stills, Posters and Designs

Designer: Roger Lightfoot

Typeset in Great Britain by Input Typesetting Ltd, London

Reprinted 1991 twice in Italy by Eurograph S.p.A. - Milan

Zachary Kwintner Books
6/7 Warren Mews
London W1P 5DJ

Introduction

'They are the most universal comics, in range as in appeal,' wrote commentator Charles Barr in the late 60s. That is as debatable a statement as one is likely to find about the Fat Man and The Thin. Nobody seemed to have an ill word to say about them as men but, as performers, their work was repetitive, variable in inspiration and quality, and many people found – and find – them desperately unfunny. Yet they enjoyed many years of huge and universal popularity and, if others were more *admired*, they were most *loved*.

The two names, Laurel and Hardy, forever linked as inextricably as sausage and mash, must be one of the century's earliest examples of the Anglo-American 'special relationship', and one of the most long-running and successful. As unlikely a pair as ever there was, it was the very contrast between them that fuelled their success.

Products of music hall and vaudeville, their humour sprang from a simple, innocent clowning that appealed to the lowest common denominator. They lacked the subtlety, grace and poetic imagination of Buster Keaton, the hard-edged brilliance of Harold Lloyd; although they hardly aspired to the range and depth of Chaplin's work, Laurel – who shared the same training ground and, on occasion, the same theatrical digs as Charlie – perhaps offered a similar appeal in his English lugubriousness, but the connection is fragile. They neither offered the pathos of Harry Langdon, nor echoed the acerbity of the great W. C. Fields. They were the last performers to take their place in the golden age of screen comedy, following in the footsteps of all the above-mentioned and, although each of them had been making silent movies for a number of years, they didn't become a team until just before the advent of the talkies, to which they seemed to adapt better than most of their illustrious contemporaries and predecessors.

Thin, red-haired Stan Laurel was born Arthur Stanley Jefferson on 16 June, 1890, in Ulverston, Lancashire. His father was a producer, actor and playwright who ran a touring theatrical company and married one of his actresses, the beautiful Madge Metcalf. In time, economic difficulties having forced a change of plan, Jefferson senior became manager of the Theatre Royal in North Shields. He went on to become a highly successful impresario in the north of England, owner of several theatres and managing director of the North British Animated Picture Company. It was hardly surprising, then, that Stan's ambition was to go on the stage, and he did so for the first time at the age of sixteen in a Glasgow music hall.

His early career followed the usual course of the time, touring the provinces with different companies until he got his lucky break from the renowned Fred Karno. He worked with and understudied Chaplin, and they both distinguished themselves – Stan, too, displaying an exceptional talent for mime – in a sketch called *Mumming Birds*. This piece was enormously successful throughout the country and in France and, in 1910, the Karno company embarked on an American tour where they presented the piece as *A Night in an English Music Hall*. A return engagement followed two years later and, this time, Stan Laurel, like Chaplin, decided to remain on American soil.

Norvell Oliver Hardy, the fifth and last child of a lawyer and local politician who died when the boy was eighteen months old, saw daylight on 18 January 1892 in Harlem, Georgia. The new baby weighed an amazing fourteen pounds at birth, and by the time he was fourteen years old, had increased this to 250. After his father's death, his mother bought a small hotel and, years later, Ollie claimed that his 'lobby watching' in childhood served as inspiration for the characters he devised with Stan. 'I used to see them in my mother's hotel when I was a kid; the dumb, dumb guy who never has anything bad happen to him – and the smart, smart guy who's dumber than the dumb guy, only he doesn't know it.' The youngster had a pretty singing voice and, at the tender age of eight, was allowed to join Coburn's Minstrels as a boy soprano. He subsequently attended the Georgia Military College where he was the butt of jokes on account of his size and, eventually, ran away. He studied singing at the Atlanta Conservatory, fell in love with moving pictures and vaudeville, and enrolled to study law at Georgia State University – a short-lived endeavour.

It was clear to all who knew him that Ollie, later known to everyone as 'Babe', was destined for show business. Helped by his mother, he bought and ran his own movie theatre and it was there that he developed an interest in silent screen comedy. In 1913 he became an extra at the Lubin Motion Picture Company in Florida, learning the business by assisting cameramen and directors and working as a script clerk.

By 1917, Stan Laurel and Oliver Hardy each had substantial independent careers – indeed, as bit player, 'heavy' and comic, Ollie had chalked up over 200 screen appearances and had even done some directing, working with Larry Semon, before joining Hal Roach's famous Comedy All-Stars. Stan had kept busy in films for Universal and for Broncho Billy Anderson before *he* joined Roach, where he completed over 50 shorts. At the Roach studios, they found themselves appearing in eleven two-reel comedies as part of the company before Roach decided to combine them as a team, and their first official Laurel and Hardy movie, *Putting Pants on Philip*, was made in 1927. Over the next three years, the duo turned out an average of one short a month, many of them directed by Leo McCarey, later to become one of Hollywood's foremost directors.

By the time they moved into feature length films, Stan and Ollie, forever recognised by their bowler hats much as Chaplin is known by his 'Little Tramp' outfit, had made over 60 short comedies together, evolving a formula of visual chaos as two gentlemanly simpletons unable to complete the most straightforward of tasks without wreaking havoc and destruction. Typical of their on-screen antics was the famous sequence in *Big Business* (1929) where they systematically destroy a house. They were essentially of the custard-pie and banana-skin school of humour, and if their inspiration periodically deserted them (Laurel, the quiet one, was the brains behind their invention), their essentially visual comedy suited the talkies well. In fact, *Music Box*, made as early as 1932, won an Oscar and demonstrated how much at ease they were with the new techniques of film-making.

It is impossible to discuss their movies in so short a biography – there were countless numbers of them – but among the best-known are *Sons of the Desert (1933), Babes in Toyland* (1934), and *The Bohemian Girl* (1936). Their last movie for Hal Roach was *Blockheads* (1938), after which their careers took a nomadic turn. They made *Flying Deuces* for RKO in 1938, then a couple more for Roach at United Artists, before embarking on several for Fox and MGM. But, alas, during the 1940s, with age creeping up on them and the demands of studio discipline becoming more rigorous, they entered a downward trend from which they would never recover. They did nothing in the late 1940s, but reunited on screen in 1951 for the last time in the French-made *Atoll K* (also known as *Robinson Crusoeland*), a failure, in which they both looked old and ill.

In private life, Stan Laurel married four times (twice to the same woman), and Oliver Hardy twice. They never accrued great wealth and, when their film careers evaporated, they worked on stage whenever they could, touring Britain during the last gasp of the music halls in 1947. In 1951, Roach sold their movies to TV for the then substantial sum of $750,000. It is reputed that the two men who helped him to his fortune received not one cent of the proceeds.

Hardy, who had appeared solo twice in supporting roles (with John Wayne in *Fighting Kentuckian*, 1949, and with Bing Crosby in *Riding High*, 1950), died of a heart attack in 1957. Stan Laurel outlived him until 1965 when he died ill and in poverty. He was, however, given a special Oscar in 1960 for his 'creative pioneering in the field of comedy' and enjoyed the small comfort of seeing their reputations rise again.

Bonnie Scotland (1935) *Metro-Goldwyn-Mayer*

The Bullfighters (1945) *20th Century-Fox*

Babes in Toyland (1934) *Metro-Goldwyn-Mayer*

Putting Pants on Philip (1927) *Metro-Goldwyn-Mayer*

Blockheads (1938) *Metro-Goldwyn-Mayer*

The Bullfighters (1945) *20th Century-Fox*

Stan Laurel and Oliver Hardy

Come Clean (1931) *Metro-Goldwyn-Mayer*

A Chump at Oxford (1940) *United Artists*

The Bullfighters (1945) *20th Century-Fox*

Bonnie Scotland (1935) *Metro-Goldwyn-Mayer*

Be Big (1930) *Metro-Goldwyn-Mayer*

Beau Hunks (1931) *Metro-Goldwyn-Mayer*

Stan Laurel and Oliver Hardy

Big Business (1929) *Metro-Goldwyn-Mayer*

The Bohemian Girl (1936) *Metro-Goldwyn-Mayer*

Great Guns (1941) *20th Century-Fox*

Below Zero (1930) *Metro-Goldwyn-Mayer*

Busy Bodies (1933) *Metro-Goldwyn-Mayer*

Stan Laurel and Oliver Hardy

The Dancing Masters (1943) *20th Century-Fox*

HR·L 31·12

Brats (1930) *Metro-Goldwyn-Mayer*

Blockheads (1938) *Metro-Goldwyn-Mayer*

Stan Laurel and Oliver Hardy

The Dancing Masters (1943) *20th Century-Fox*

The Big Noise (1944) *20th Century-Fox*

Oliver Hardy

Babes in Toyland (1934) *Metro-Goldwyn-Mayer*

Chickens Come Home (1931) *Metro-Goldwyn-Mayer*

Oliver Hardy

Zenobia (1939) *Metro-Goldwyn-Mayer*

Call of the Cuckoo (1927) *Metro-Goldwyn-Mayer*

Angora Love (1929) *Metro-Goldwyn-Mayer*

Stan Laurel and Oliver Hardy

The Chimp (1932) *Metro-Goldwyn-Mayer*

Stan Laurel and Oliver Hardy

Double Whoopee (1929) *Metro-Goldwyn-Mayer*

Laughing Gravy (1931) *Metro-Goldwyn-Mayer*

You're Darn Tootin' (1928) *Metro-Goldwyn-Mayer*

Stan Laurel and Oliver Hardy

Berth Marks (1929) *Metro-Goldwyn-Mayer*

Way Out West (1937) *Metro-Goldwyn-Mayer*

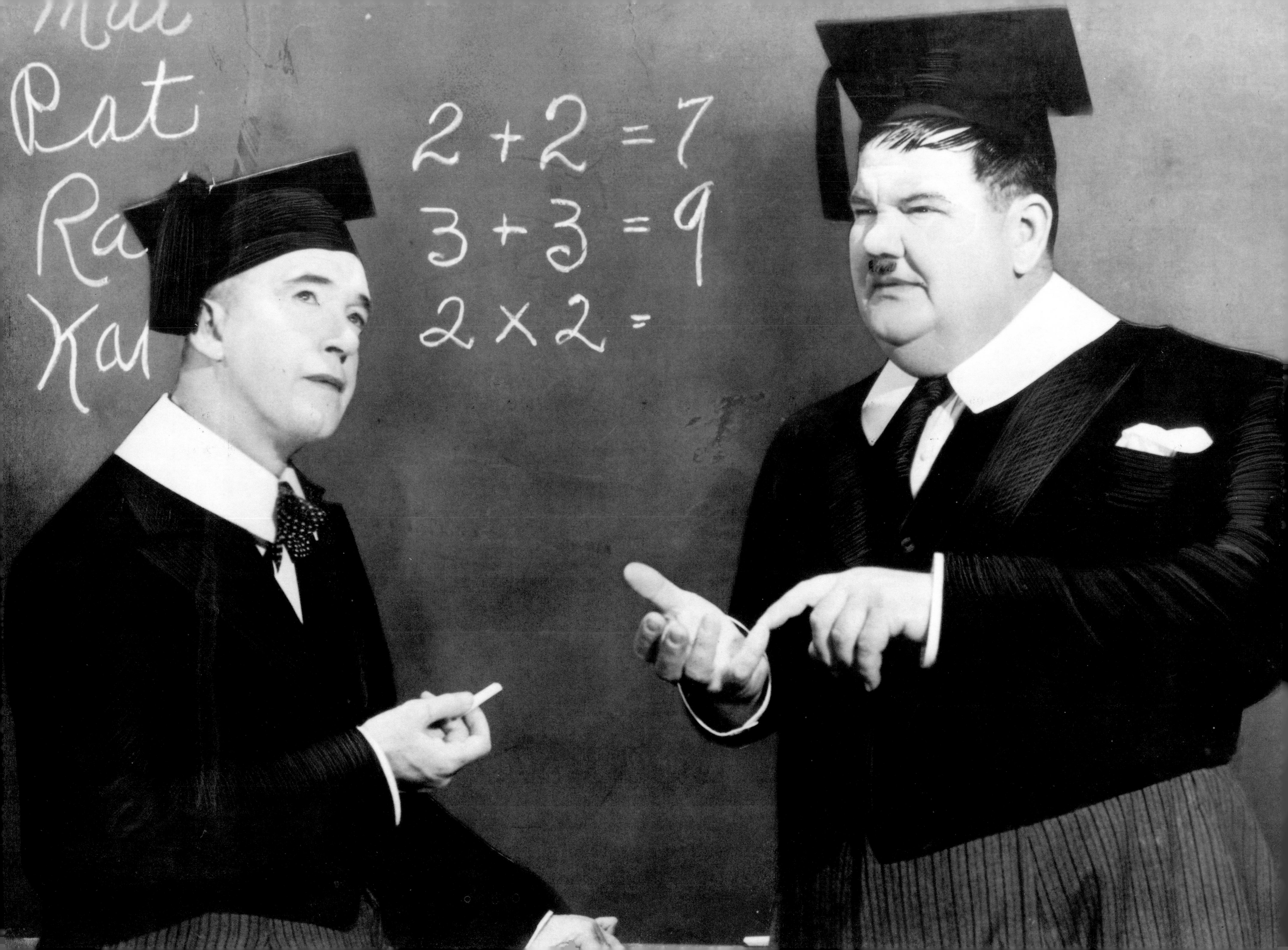
Rat
2+2=7
3+3=9
2×2=

A Chump at Oxford (1940) *United Artists*

The Battle of the Century (1927) *Metro-Goldwyn-Mayer*

Stan Laurel and Oliver Hardy

Reprinted 1991 in Italy by
Eurograph S.p.A. - Milan